Roberto Alomar

Additional Titles in the Sports Reports *Series*

Andre Agassi
Star Tennis Player
(0-89490-798-0)

Troy Aikman
Star Quarterback
(0-89490-927-4)

Roberto Alomar
Star Second Baseman
(0-7660-1079-1)

Charles Barkley
Star Forward
(0-89490-655-0)

Jeff Gordon
Star Race Car Driver
(0-7660-1083-X)

Wayne Gretzky
Star Center
(0-89490-930-4)

Ken Griffey, Jr.
Star Outfielder
(0-89490-802-2)

Scott Hamilton
Star Figure Skater
(0-7660-1236-0)

Anfernee Hardaway
Star Guard
(0-7660-1234-4)

Grant Hill
Star Forward
(0-7660-1078-3)

Shawn Kemp
Star Forward
(0-89490-929-0)

Mario Lemieux
Star Center
(0-89490-932-0)

Karl Malone
Star Forward
(0-89490-931-2)

Dan Marino
Star Quarterback
(0-89490-933-9)

Mark Messier
Star Center
(0-89490-801-4)

Reggie Miller
Star Guard
(0-7660-1082-1)

Chris Mullin
Star Forward
(0-89490-486-8)

Hakeem Olajuwon
Star Center
(0-89490-803-0)

Shaquille O'Neal
Star Center
(0-89490-656-9)

Scottie Pippen
Star Forward
(0-7660-1080-5)

David Robinson
Star Center
(0-89490-483-3)

Barry Sanders
Star Running Back
(0-89490-484-1)

Deion Sanders
Star Athlete
(0-89490-652-6)

Junior Seau
Star Linebacker
(0-89490-800-6)

Emmitt Smith
Star Running Back
(0-89490-653-4)

Frank Thomas
Star First Baseman
(0-89490-659-3)

Thurman Thomas
Star Running Back
(0-89490-445-0)

Chris Webber
Star Forward
(0-89490-799-9)

Tiger Woods
Star Golfer
(0-7660-1081-3)

Steve Young
Star Quarterback
(0-89490-654-2)

Michael Jordan
Star Guard
(0-89490-482-5)

Jim Kelly
Star Quarterback
(0-89490-446-9)

Jerry Rice
Star Wide Receiver
(0-89490-928-2)

Cal Ripken, Jr.
Star Shortstop
(0-89490-485-X)

SPORTS REPORTS

Roberto Alomar

Star Second Baseman

Stew Thornley

Enslow Publishers, Inc.

44 Fadem Road   PO Box 38
Box 699   Aldershot
Springfield, NJ 07081   Hants GU12 6BP
USA   UK

http://www.enslow.com

Library of Congress Cataloging-in-Publication Data

Thornley, Stew.
     Roberto Alomar : star second baseman / Stew Thornley.
        p. cm. — (Sports Reports)
     Includes bibliographical references (p.) and index.
     Summary: Discusses the personal life and professional career of the Puerto
Rican-born all-star baseball player, Roberto Alomar.
     ISBN 0-7660-1079-1
     1. Alomar, Roberto, 1968- —Juvenile literature. 2. Baseball players—Puerto
Rico—Biography—Juvenile literature. [1. Alomar, Roberto, 1968– . 2. Baseball
players. 3. Puerto Ricans—Biography.] I. Title II. Series
GV865.S37Y56 1999
796.357′092—dc21
    [B]   98-13667
                                                    CIP
                                                      AC

Printed in the United States of America.

10 9 8 7 6 5 4 3 2 1

Photo Credits: Charleston River Dogs, p. 24; Courtesy of Anaheim Angels,
p. 13; Enslow Publishers, Inc., p. 85; New York Mets, p. 93; Ron Vesely, pp.
38, 43, 45, 49, 52, 64, 71, 75, 79, 81; Stew Thornley, pp. 15, 18, 19, 27, 35, 62,
66, 88.

Cover Photo: Ron Vesely

Contents

1 Focus on Baseball 7

2 Childhood Years 11

3 Baseball Throughout the Year 23

4 Pride of the Padres 31

5 Reaching the Top 41

6 Rocky Roads 57

7 New Challenges 69

8 Born to Play Baseball 84

Chapter Notes 95

Career Statistics 99

Where to Write 101

Index 103

Chapter 1

Focus on Baseball

Only twelve players in the history of major-league baseball have ever hit four home runs in one game. Roberto Alomar, star second baseman for the Baltimore Orioles, almost joined that elite group as he hit a deep fly to right field during a game against the Boston Red Sox on April 26, 1997.

Alomar was not even trying to go deep in his first four at-bats. But he was thinking about a home run as he came to bat in the seventh inning. So were the forty-seven thousand fans in attendance at Oriole Park. They cheered loudly as Alomar stepped into the batter's box, hoping he could hit another one out.

It was not long enough to clear the fence and was caught; however, it was deep enough to allow Mike

Bordick to tag up at third base and score. This gave Alomar his sixth run batted in (RBI) of the game. He admitted he was trying for more. "I was in the zone. . . . The fourth time, yeah, I was thinking home run."[1]

Baltimore had won 13 of its first 19 games and was in first place going into the game against the Red Sox on Saturday, April 26. A Gold Glove second baseman, Alomar is also one of baseball's best hitters. Year after year, he has been voted to the American League All-Star team. In the early 1990s he played on two world championship teams with the Toronto Blue Jays. In 1996 he switched to the Baltimore Orioles and played a key role in helping the team make the playoffs.

Alomar is used to having good times associated with baseball. Growing up in Puerto Rico, he focused on little else, and it was this focus that helped make him as good as he is. But Alomar had to battle to maintain his focus during the first month of the 1997 season.

His fielding was as good as ever, and he continued to thrill Oriole fans with his spectacular plays in the field. However, he was struggling at the plate.

During the winter, Alomar had severely injured his left ankle, playing in a charity basketball game in Puerto Rico. The injury was affecting his hitting.

When he batted left-handed, he had trouble putting weight on his back foot.

Alomar was happy his team was doing so well, but he was eager to start contributing to its success. His batting average was only .205, nearly 100 points below his career average. But he felt good as he took batting practice and had a feeling he was in for a good game.[2]

The Orioles would need it. They fell behind 3–0 in the top of the first inning. But in the bottom of the inning, Alomar put Baltimore on the scoreboard. He singled and later came home on a hit by teammate Cal Ripken.

When Alomar came to bat in the second inning, Boston was ahead 4–3. Brady Anderson was on first base when Alomar lifted a long fly down the left-field line for a two-run homer. Not only did the blow put his team ahead 5–4, it was the one hundredth home run of his career. But Alomar did not stop there. He homered again in the fourth inning, and then, in the fifth—with Anderson on base again—he connected for another home run. The Orioles went on to win the game, 14–5.

Alomar's slump was broken, and he knew good times were in front of him again.

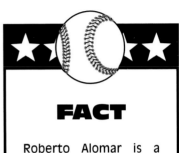

FACT

Roberto Alomar is a switch-hitter, meaning he can bat either right-handed or left-handed. Right-handed batters usually do better against left-handed pitchers and vice versa. Switch-hitting gives a player an advantage because he can choose which side of the plate to hit from, depending on whether the pitcher is right- or left-handed. It also helps because a curve ball will break toward rather than away from a batter.

Chapter 2

Childhood Years

Raising a family can be difficult for professional baseball players because they spend a lot of time away from home during the season. When the home is Puerto Rico, it can be even tougher. Roberto's brother, Sandy Alomar, Jr., was born June 18, 1966. Roberto was born February 5, 1968, in Ponce, Puerto Rico. When their father, Sandy Alomar, Sr., would leave for the United States each spring, their mother, Maria, would stay behind to take care of their growing family. Eventually she was able to pack up the kids and join her husband in the United States for part of the season.

Such a lifestyle can be difficult for a player's family, as well. But while there are challenges in this, there can be advantages. Roberto and his brother had opportunities that other kids would love to have. They hung out with their father in a major-league clubhouse and mingled with other players. Both enjoyed it, but Roberto was especially taken by the experience. At the age of two, he could identify all his father's California Angels teammates by their uniform numbers.

Roberto was comfortable at a baseball stadium. He enjoyed becoming friendly with his father's teammates and with their children. Away from the ballpark, though, it was a little different. It was not easy shuttling between Puerto Rico and the United States mainland every year. For the Alomar children, it meant having to make new friends on the mainland every year. This was no problem for Roberto's brother, Sandy. He spoke English better than Roberto did.

At the end of each summer, Roberto's mother returned to Puerto Rico with Roberto and his brother, while their father played out the rest of the season on the mainland. When that season ended, Roberto's father rejoined his family in Puerto Rico and continued to play ball over the winter.

Back in Puerto Rico, Roberto had just as much of a craving for baseball. He accompanied his dad when he played in the Puerto Rican League. During the 1970–71 winter season, his father had won the

Even at age two, Roberto Alomar could identify all of his father's California Angels teammates. Sandy Alomar, Sr., is shown here as a member of the Angels.

batting title. He was also named the league's Most Valuable Player. Roberto's father played for the Ponce Leones at that time. Roberto would hurry home from school each day, making sure he got there in time to get in the car and go with his dad as he went off to another game.

At the ballpark, Roberto worked out with the other players before the games. He would participate in infield drills with them and was even able to take a little batting practice if he could get someone to pitch to him. Once the games started, Roberto often served as the batboy for his father's team.

Of course, Roberto was doing more than just tagging along. He was playing baseball himself and showing great ability at an early age.

There is no question that Roberto's father had passed on a lot of his baseball skill and experience to his sons. One of the things he urged them to do was to become a switch-hitter just as he was. "I wanted to create that type of talent in them," he said, adding that he told them that switch-hitting would "be an advantage for a player who wants to play every day."[1] Both Sandy junior and Roberto followed their father's advice, although Sandy junior gave up the practice before he reached the major leagues.

"Robby was born to play baseball," said his father.[2] In fact, Roberto's constant companions—even

before he was out of diapers—were a baseball cap, glove, and bat. When his parents asked him what he wanted for Christmas each year, the request was always the same—a new bat and ball.

Roberto would take his equipment outside and find other boys to play with. The games were often played in the streets, although any vacant lot could also serve as a baseball diamond. The Monserrate neighborhood of Salinas, Puerto Rico, had lots of young couples, like Roberto's parents, raising young families. There was no shortage of playmates for Roberto, and there was no shortage of adults to supervise him. The neighborhood was like one large extended family for all the children in it.

Roberto Alomar did more than just tag along to watch his father play baseball. Roberto started playing baseball in Puerto Rico as a young boy. A stadium in Salinas, Puerto Rico, is shown here.

While Roberto could never get enough baseball, his brother did not maintain the same passion for the game. Sandy junior liked baseball and played it as he grew up. He did not have the grace of his brother to be a slick infielder, so he took up catching instead. But as he got older, Sandy junior developed an interest in a number of other sports, such as Tae Kwon Do, surfing, volleyball, and dirt biking. By the time he was thirteen, he even quit playing baseball for a while.

Roberto, however, never strayed. He began playing in formal youth leagues when he was seven and was always the best player at his level, even though some of the players were older than he was. He loved baseball so much that his parents found an easy way to punish him if he misbehaved—they would take his bat and glove away from him.[3]

Whether playing in pickup games on the sandlot or in the organized leagues, Roberto Alomar was attracting a lot of attention, even though he was only eleven years old.

By this time, Roberto's father was wrapping up his career as a player on the mainland. He stayed involved in the Puerto Rican League for a while longer. He managed and played for the Ponce Leones during the 1980–81 winter season, but then he left baseball completely.

Some players have trouble getting used to life after baseball. In this case, it was Roberto who had difficulty adjusting. On one hand, he could spend more time with his dad. His dad no longer had to leave the family in the spring to go to the mainland. On the other hand, Roberto missed having a father who was a major-league baseball player.

Roberto's dad would get involved in baseball again, but for the time being, he decided to go into business. He bought and operated a gas station in Salinas, Puerto Rico. He did not make as much money as he had while playing baseball, and the Alomar family struggled financially. Roberto learned what it was like to be poor. It was a lesson he remembered even after he got to the major leagues and signed contracts worth millions. He still knew the value of a dollar and was not one to spend money carelessly, no matter how much he had.

As for Roberto's brother, he had been involved in many activities but eventually found his way back to baseball. Sandy Alomar, Jr., began catching for an American Legion team and found himself enjoying the game as he never had before. He was doing well and drawing notice from scouts from the mainland. Scouts are employed by major-league teams to find and evaluate good young ballplayers.

One of the scouts who saw Roberto's brother

play was Luis Rosa. He was a family friend who was influential in Latin American baseball. Rosa had scouted for various major-league teams. He was working for the San Diego Padres at the time the Alomar boys were getting old enough to think about professional contracts. At that time, Puerto Rican players had a choice of major-league organizations to sign with. Puerto Rico was still "open territory." Its players were not subject to a free-agent draft as players on the mainland were. A draft is held each year among mainland players who have never

Roberto Alomar grew up in the Monserrate neighborhood of Salinas, Puerto Rico. He was always able to find friends there to play baseball.

signed a professional contract. All the major-league teams take turns drafting these players for their organizations. A good young player coming out of high school or college in Texas, Pennsylvania, or Florida does not have much of a choice. Such a player may want to play for the New York Yankees or the Cincinnati Reds; however, he cannot choose. He has to sign with the organization that drafts him or not sign at all.

But during the time that Puerto Rico was open territory, its players could choose the organization

Roberto Alomar grew up in Salinas, Puerto Rico. When Roberto's father decided to go into business for himself, he bought a gas station in Salinas.

they wanted to be a part of. Because of Luis Rosa, the Padres had a connection to some of the top players in Puerto Rico, including the Alomars. Roberto was considered the better baseball player of the two brothers. But he was still too young to sign a pro contract. Meanwhile, Sandy junior was also a good prospect, and the Padres signed him to a contract in October 1983, when he was just seventeen.

Sandy junior played for the Padres' minor-league team in Spokane, Washington, in 1984. He was a catcher, but he also played some games at first base. He was a switch-hitter when he broke into pro ball. However, he struggled trying to hit from both sides of the plate and eventually became solely a right-handed batter.

Because the Padres already had Sandy Alomar, Jr., the organization figured to have the inside track with Roberto. The team found a way to sweeten the pot a little more. They knew that Roberto and Sandy junior's father wanted to get back into baseball. They also knew that he was a knowledgeable baseball man who could help some of their young players. So the Padres offered the boys' dad a job in their organization as a minor-league coach. He was happy to get out of the gas-station business and back into baseball.

Eleven days past his seventeenth birthday,

FACT

Despite all the time he spent on ball fields—either playing himself or attending games in which his father was playing—Roberto Alomar was a good student. He brought his books along and found time to study in the clubhouse before his father's winter-league games.

Roberto Alomar signed a contract with the San Diego Padres. He was in the process of completing high school, and his teachers gave him special tests so that he could graduate early and be ready to start on a baseball career.[4]

In the spring of 1985, Roberto's father packed his bags to go to the Padres' minor-league complex in Yuma, Arizona. A trip to the mainland for the start of a baseball season was nothing new. But this time it would be different. This time his sons would be with him. And they would no longer be just tagging along. This time they would be playing.

Chapter 3

Baseball Throughout the Year

The arrival of the three Alomars in Yuma represented a different phase in the life of each one. For Roberto's father, it marked a return to baseball after several years away from it. For Roberto's brother, it was a continuation of a pro career that had begun the year before. For Roberto, it was a completely new stage as, for the first time, he was now playing baseball for a living.

Roberto had been to the mainland many times before but never on his own. And for his first year in organized ball, at least, he would still have his family around. Not only did the Alomar men spend spring training together, they all went to the same place when the season started. That place was Charleston, South Carolina. All would be

In his first year of organized baseball in the United States, Roberto Alomar (jumping into the air) played for the Charleston Rainbows.

members—Roberto's father as coach, his brother as catcher, and Roberto as second baseman—of the Charleston Rainbows of the South Atlantic League. The Rainbows were a Class-A team in the Padres' farm system, a place for young prospects to get started. If players did well, they would move up the chain and get closer to the major leagues. All three Alomars lived in the same house in Charleston and, that summer, were joined by Roberto's mother.

For many players, the start of a baseball career marks their first time away from home. In addition to pressures they face on the field, they have to contend with homesickness. For players coming from Latin America, it can be extremely difficult. Their families are even farther away, and they have to struggle to adapt to a new culture without them. But for Roberto, the transition was much easier. He was still with his brother and parents, and he had lived on the mainland before. "It helped me having my family there," he said, "because I was the youngest one in the family. If I had been by myself, I would have been lost."[1]

Roberto did well offensively but struggled in the field. He led the South Atlantic League by playing in 137 games and having 546 at-bats. His batting average was .293, which was good. However, he also led the league by making 35 errors at second base. It was apparent he needed a lot of improvement in that area.

Both Roberto and Sandy junior played in the South Atlantic League All-Star Game that summer. Roberto was even listed as the best young second-base prospect in baseball in *Baseball America* magazine.

It was also a good season for the boys' father. He did well enough that he landed a coaching job in the major leagues by the following season. It would be a few more years before his sons would join him at that level.

Following the 1985 season on the mainland, Roberto returned home—but not to rest. He would be playing winter baseball in the Puerto Rican League, with the Caguas Criollos.

Roberto had a fine manager to play for in Caguas—Felipe Alou, who later became manager of the Montreal Expos. Alomar started the season as a backup to Al Newman at second base. But Alou found a way to work Alomar into the regular lineup: He moved Newman to shortstop and put Alomar in at second base. Alomar helped Caguas finish the regular season with the best record in the league. However, a playoff is held among the top four teams in the league to determine the championship. The Mayaguez Indios ended up winning the title and advancing to the Caribbean Series (a series against the league champions from Mexico, Venezuela, and the Dominican Republic).

Back on the mainland in 1986, Roberto Alomar spent the season with the Reno, Nevada, team (in the California League) and showed great improvement. His .346 batting average was the best in the league. He also cut his errors nearly in half from the year before.

He kept going in the winter, playing for Caguas again. The Criollos won the Puerto Rican League

When Roberto Alomar returned to Puerto Rico following the 1985 baseball season on the mainland, he played in Caguas, Puerto Rico. The stadium in Caguas is shown here.

title and went on to win the Caribbean Series, which was played in Hermosillo, Mexico.

When the 1987 mainland season opened, both Roberto and his brother were assigned to play with the Wichita Wranglers (in Wichita, Kansas) in the Class-AA Texas League. Roberto Alomar had a new position, however—shortstop. The Padres were looking for someone to take the spot of Garry Templeton, their current shortstop, who was thinking about retiring within the next couple of seasons.

It was not an easy move for Alomar. After having made such progress in his fielding at second base in 1986, he was back to struggling defensively. He made 36 errors at shortstop, the most in the league. The Padres decided to move him back to second base. It was a wise choice, as Alomar would develop into the top second baseman in all of baseball.

Although he had a frustrating year in the field with Wichita, Alomar once again performed well at the plate. He hit .319 with 12 home runs. He also had 41 doubles, second in the league.

After another winter with Caguas in the Puerto Rican League, where Alomar hit .302 and had 14 stolen bases, he returned to Yuma, Arizona, in the spring of 1988. This time, though, he trained with the major-league Padres rather than spend his time in their minor-league complex. This did not mean he

FACT

The Puerto Rican League holds a draft for native players, and Roberto was drafted by the Arecibo Lobos. Arecibo was the farthest city in the league from the Alomar home in Salinas. Roberto's father did not want his son playing so far away. Alomar was traded and ended up as a member of the Caguas Criollos. Caguas is seventeen miles south of San Juan and approximately thirty miles northeast of Salinas.

would be in the majors when the season opened, but to be in the major-league training camp was encouraging.

The Padres were in need of help at several positions. The path to a spot on the Padres was open for Alomar. The leading candidates to play second base were Randy Ready and Tim Flannery. Alomar hoped he could win the job.

He worked hard during spring training and caught the eye of a number of people, including Tony Gwynn, the Padres' great hitter. Gwynn was impressed with Roberto Alomar's determination. When the exhibition season opened, Alomar dazzled even more people. He made a number of spectacular plays in the field and had a batting average of .385 through his first nine games. His hopes soared that he could stay with the Padres when the regular season began.

However, the Padres had been burned in previous attempts to fill the second-base spot with youngsters. They knew Alomar was going to be a great player but did not want to rush him. If they brought him up before he was ready, it could destroy his confidence and hurt his career. Padres manager Larry Bowa discussed the decision with his coaching staff, which included Roberto's father, who said little. It was hard for him to separate his roles as coach and

FACT

During spring training in 1987, Roberto Alomar roomed with Carlos Baerga, another Puerto Rican who had been signed by Luis Rosa. Baerga would go on to several fine seasons at second base with the Cleveland Indians in the 1990s. He later became a teammate of Alomar's in the Puerto Rican League.

father in this situation, so he left it to the others to decide. In the end, the Padres figured that a little additional training for Roberto Alomar, at the Class AAA level, could not hurt.

Roberto Alomar felt differently when he was told he would be starting the season with the Las Vegas Stars in the Pacific Coast League rather than with the San Diego Padres in the National League. He was hoping so much to make it to the majors that he was devastated when he did not.

However, he did not sulk or complain. He went to Las Vegas determined to do well so that his stay there would be brief. It was. Alomar drove in 14 runs in his first 9 games. Meanwhile, the Padres were struggling. The team lost its first five games of the season and knew it was in need of help. It was apparent by this time that Roberto Alomar could provide that help.

Chapter 4

Pride of the Padres

Just twenty-three days after being told he would be starting the season in Las Vegas, Roberto Alomar got the call he was waiting for. He was going up to the major leagues. Alomar joined the Padres in Los Angeles for a series with the Dodgers, but he had to wait a few days before seeing any action. When he arrived, Los Angeles was experiencing several days of rain. The final three games of the Padres-Dodgers series were rained out, an extremely rare event for Los Angeles.

The Padres headed home to San Diego to open a three-game series against the Houston Astros. Alomar was familiar with the pitcher he would face in his first major-league game: It was Nolan Ryan, who had once played for the California Angels with

Roberto's father. As for Roberto's father, he was standing in the third-base coaching box as his son came to bat in the bottom of the first inning. The count reached two balls and two strikes when Ryan delivered a curve ball. Roberto Alomar reached out and hit a grounder in the hole between shortstop and third base. Third baseman Denny Walling was able to glove the ball but had no chance of throwing the speedy Alomar out at first. Alomar kept the ball as a souvenir of his first hit in the majors. He did not score that inning, but the Padres were able to build a 3–1 lead over the Astros on a solo home run by Marvell Wynne in the fourth inning and a two-run homer by Benito Santiago in the sixth.

San Diego still led in the ninth inning, but the Astros got the lead-off batter on base, bringing the tying run to the plate. However, Alomar snuffed the rally. He grabbed a ground ball, stepped on second base to force out the runner, then fired to first to complete the double play. Thanks to that gorgeous play the Padres held on for a 3–1 win.

Alomar had two hits in the next game as San Diego won again. In the final game of the series, the score was tied 0–0 when Alomar came to bat in the fifth inning. Teammate Dickie Thon was on second base. Alomar broke up the scoreless duel with a single that brought Thon home. The Padres went on to a 3–0 win as San Diego right-hander Andy Hawkins held Houston to only one hit.

Following the sweep of the Astros, the Padres won again in their next game. However, they then lost 21 of their next 29 games and Larry Bowa was let go. Jack McKeon took over as manager, and the Padres eventually rebounded. After the rough start, they were able to finish the season in third place in the National League Western Division with a win-loss record of 83–78.

Roberto Alomar was one of the reasons the Padres did so well over the last half of the season. He hit .316 in his final 55 games and played well at second base. Of course, the Padres had other good players, including Tony Gwynn, who won his third batting title, leading the National League with a .313 average. Benito Santiago slumped a bit with his bat but still did an outstanding job on defense as catcher. It was because Santiago did so well that Roberto's brother remained stuck in the minors, even though he hit .297 at Las Vegas.

For Roberto Alomar, his rookie season had been a success. His batting average of .266 was second on the team, behind only Gwynn, and he led the Padres with 84 runs scored. Alomar kept up his good play that winter, hitting .314 for Caguas in the Puerto Rican League.

FACT

Even though he made a lot of errors at second base early in his career, Roberto Alomar was still regarded as a good fielder because of his great range. He was able to make plays on many ground balls that most second basemen would not be able to get to. He showed remarkable grace in the infield and started to develop what became his signature play: going to his right for a grounder up the middle, sliding on one knee as he backhanded the ball, then popping up and making a perfect throw to first in one fluid motion.

Back on the mainland for the 1989 season, Roberto Alomar—at the age of twenty-one—was the youngest player on any opening-day roster in the National League. He was getting a chance to start the season with the Padres and was anxious to do his best—perhaps too anxious. He made 11 errors in the first month. "I was too aggressive then because I wanted to make every play," he explained.[1] Alomar settled down but still led the National League in errors at second base.

On offense, though, Alomar sparkled. He raised his batting average to .295 and was third in the league with 184 hits. He was also a threat on the basepaths, finishing second in the league with 42 stolen bases. With good seasons from Alomar and Gwynn, who won his third straight batting title, the Padres moved up to second place. The team finished only three games behind the San Francisco Giants in the Western Division.

At the end of the 1989 major-league season, Alomar experienced a trade—in the Puerto Rican League. The Caguas Criollos traded Alomar—for young slugger Juan Gonzalez—to the Ponce Leones, a team managed by Alomar's father. Alomar did not play long for his father, though. He had a number of nagging injuries and took part in only 17 games. It would be his last appearance in the Puerto Rican

At the end of 1989, Roberto Alomar was traded—in the Puerto Rican League. He went from the Caguas Criollos to the Ponce Leones. The stadium in Ponce, Puerto Rico, is shown here.

League for several years, as he concentrated solely on baseball on the mainland over the next few seasons.

The 1990 season was a difficult one for the Padres. The team dropped to fourth place after having finished within three games of the top spot the previous year. There was a great deal of turmoil in the front office, which may have been a reason for the Padres' poor performance. The team changed ownership in June, and the following month, after having lost 14 of 19 games, changed managers. Greg Riddoch took over as manager from Jack McKeon but did not do much better as the Padres lost 11 of their first 12 games under him.

There was at least one bright spot for Roberto Alomar during this time. He got the chance to play in his first All-Star Game. He was selected as a backup at second base for the National League. He got into the game in the late innings, replacing Ryne Sandberg of the Chicago Cubs, and flied out in his only at-bat. The All-Star Game was another family affair for the Alomars. Roberto's father was there as a coach, and his brother made it as the starting catcher for the American League.

Things did not go well for Roberto Alomar and his father over the rest of the year. Neither got along well with the new manager. Riddoch made some

FACT

Roberto's brother, Sandy Alomar, Jr., had another good year in the minor leagues in 1989. For the second straight season, he was named Player of the Year in the Pacific Coast League. The San Diego front office knew that Sandy junior was too good to keep in the minor leagues. At the end of the season, the Padres traded him to the Cleveland Indians. The move to Cleveland gave Sandy junior the chance to show that he could be a star in the major leagues.

negative remarks to the press about Roberto. Alomar was trying his hardest and was hurt to see such comments in the paper. Even though the team was slumping, the Padres announced that Riddoch would be back again in 1991. Roberto's father figured that signaled the end of his days with the team. He was right. At the end of the season he was let go. He ended up with the Chicago Cubs, working as an infield instructor with the organization's minor-league teams.

There was now only one Alomar left in San Diego. That did not last long, however. In December 1990 the Padres pulled off a blockbuster deal with the Toronto Blue Jays of the American League. Roberto Alomar and outfielder Joe Carter were traded to Toronto for first baseman Fred McGriff and shortstop Tony Fernandez. Carter and McGriff were great sluggers and Fernandez was one of the top shortstops in the game. They were the big names in the deal, but many experts predicted that Alomar would end up as the best player of them all.

The trade took Roberto Alomar away from the turmoil in San Diego, but he was not happy to leave. He loved southern California and had purchased a home on the ocean. As for Toronto, Alomar did not know much about the city other than it is in Canada, and it is cold.

In December 1990, Roberto Alomar was traded from the San Diego Padres to the Toronto Blue Jays. He did not know much about Toronto, Canada, but he soon found it to be just like other cities.

As a member of the Padres, Roberto Alomar had played some games in Montreal, a part of Canada that is French-speaking. He thought Toronto would be like Montreal and that he would have to adjust to still another culture. When he got to Toronto, though, he found that it was not that much different from any other large city in the United States.

There was one major difference, though. Toronto was a hockey town. The sports heroes in that city were normally members of the Toronto Maple Leafs of the National Hockey League. It would not take long for Roberto Alomar to change that.

Chapter 5

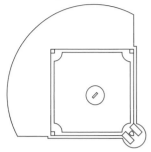

Reaching the Top

Roberto Alomar settled in quite well in Toronto. To say he lived near the ballpark would be an understatement; it would be more accurate to say he lived in the ballpark. Actually, he lived in a suite in the hotel that was attached to SkyDome, the Blue Jays' stadium.

SkyDome, which opened in 1989, was the first stadium to have a retractable roof. (Montreal's stadium was revamped in 1989 to have a retractable roof, but the roof never worked and remained closed.) The roof could be closed when the weather was bad and left open when it was nice. But the magnificence of SkyDome extended to more than its roof. The structure was huge and included restaurants and the hotel, which overlooked the playing area. It would be possible for a guest in the SkyDome Hotel to watch the game from the comfort of a room. Of course, this feature was one Alomar did not care about. He would have a field-level view for the games.

The Blue Jays had high hopes in 1991. They had put together a number of good teams in previous years but had not yet reached the World Series. In 1985 and 1989 they had won the American League Eastern Division title but had been beaten each year in the league playoffs. In 1990 they had finished two games out of first place in the Eastern Division.

The Blue Jays got off to a quick start in 1991, winning six of their first eight games, before faltering toward the end of April. They started off May not only with a loss to the Texas Rangers, but also without getting a single hit. They were the victims of Nolan Ryan's seventh career no-hitter. Alomar was prominent in the game as Ryan struck him out to finish off the no-hitter. Three years before, Alomar had collected his first major-league hit off Ryan and kept the ball as a souvenir; this time it was Ryan's turn to keep the souvenir ball.

Once past this game, however, the Blue Jays—and Alomar—began turning it on. Alomar was named the Blue Jays' Player of the Month in May. The Blue Jays climbed to second place, staying close

Roberto Alomar and his Blue Jays teammates started 1991 with high hopes for a championship season.

to the top spot and finally moving into first place in early June. By the All-Star break in July, the Blue Jays had opened up a lead of five and a half games over the Boston Red Sox.

There was so much baseball excitement in Toronto in 1991 that the Blue Jays ended up with a season total of more than 4 million in attendance. Never before had a major-league team drawn more than 4 million fans in a single season.

Alomar was a big part of the excitement that was helping his team steal some of the sports thunder from the NHL's Maple Leafs. Roberto Alomar had become the dominant Alomar in baseball.

Alomar had a batting average of .295 and scored 88 runs during the regular season. He also gained recognition for his fielding. For the first time, he won a Gold Glove, signifying that he was the best fielding second baseman in the league. Most important to Alomar, though, was that the Blue Jays finished in first place in the American League Eastern Division. They would face the Minnesota Twins in a best-of-seven series to see who would advance to the World Series.

Alomar had an outstanding playoff series as he led both teams with a .474 average and had four runs batted in (RBIs) over five games. Unfortunately, the rest of the team did not do as well. Minnesota

The Blue Jays—and Roberto Alomar—had a good season in 1991. By the All-Star break in July, the team had moved into first place with a lead of five and a half games over the Boston Red Sox.

FACT

Roberto Alomar played in the All-Star Game in 1991. This time, however, it was for the American League. He was in the starting lineup as a result of receiving the most votes among American League second basemen. Sandy junior also started for the American League as catcher. This marked the first time brothers had ever been a member of the same starting lineup in an All-Star Game. The All-Star Game was played at SkyDome, and more than fifty-two thousand fans were on hand to see the American League win 4–2.

defeated Toronto, four games to one, handing the Blue Jays another frustrating end to their season.

The determination to do better in 1992 extended from the players all the way up to the Toronto front office. General manager Pat Gillick went into the free-agent market to sign a number of players who could make the Blue Jays even stronger. (A free agent is a player whose contract with his current team has expired.) Jack Morris, who pitched for the Twins in 1991, was one of those free agents. One of the top right-handed pitchers in the American League, Morris had won two games against the Blue Jays in the playoffs. He then won two more games in the World Series and was named the World Series Most Valuable Player. Alomar and the rest of the Blue Jays were happy that Morris would be pitching for them (rather than against them).

Another free agent—veteran slugger Dave Winfield—also signed with the Blue Jays for 1992. Pat Gillick signed free agents from other teams as well, but he was aware that some of his own players could eventually become free agents. One player he wanted to keep was Roberto Alomar, and he knew the way to do it was with a long-term contract. On February 7, 1992, Alomar signed a three-year contract worth $18.5 million. At the time, it made him the best-paid second baseman in baseball.

Alomar responded to the Blue Jays' faith in him by getting off to a fast start in 1992. He was named Player of the Month in the American League in April and followed that up with another good month in May. In June, Alomar sprained his left knee sliding home in a game at Yankee Stadium in New York and missed five games. When he returned to the lineup, though, he came back strong, driving in four runs in a game against the Detroit Tigers.

The All-Star Game was coming up, and once again, the Alomar brothers would be starting for the American League. It was a homecoming of sorts for Roberto and his brother because the game was played in San Diego. Each had a hit in the game as the American League rolled to a 13–6 win. Roberto's hit was a single to lead off the second inning. He then stole second and third base before being driven home by his Toronto teammate Joe Carter. The two stolen bases in one inning set an All-Star Game record.

Alomar did a good job stealing bases throughout the season. Over a span of nearly two months, from late June to mid-August, he stole 17 bases in a row without being thrown out. His streak was snapped in a game at Cleveland. The catcher who threw him out was his brother.

Alomar was not the only Blue Jay having an

outstanding season. The newcomers, Morris and Winfield, contributed greatly to the team's success. Morris won 21 games during the regular season. He was the first Toronto pitcher ever to win at least 20 games in a year. Winfield came through with 26 home runs and 108 RBIs to go with a .290 batting average. Joe Carter did even better with 34 home runs and 119 RBIs.

Even so, Alomar was named the team's Player of the Year by the Toronto chapter of the Baseball Writers Association of America. He scored 105 runs and hit .310. His batting average was even better with runners in scoring position. With a runner on second or third, Alomar hit .354. When the bases were loaded, his average was .444.

Again, Alomar was at his best in the field. He made only 5 errors at second base (tying an American League record for fewest errors at that position over a full season) and won his second straight Gold Glove.

With performances like these, it was no surprise that the Blue Jays finished first in the American League East. There was little celebration over the division title, however. They had done this before. If they could not at least win the American League playoffs and get to the World Series, the team would not consider the season a success.

In 1992, Roberto Alomar was at his best in the field. He won his second straight Gold Glove.

They would face the American League West champions, the Oakland Athletics. The teams split the first two games, which were played in Toronto. The series then went west for three games at Oakland.

Toronto won the third game 7–5 to take the lead in the series, but it looked as if Oakland would tie it up as the Athletics held a 6–1 lead after seven innings in Game 4. Alomar was not ready to quit, though. He led off the eighth inning with a double. That hit was the start of a three-run rally for the Blue Jays that cut the Athletics' lead to 6–4.

In the ninth, Devon White singled to open the inning for the Blue Jays. Alomar stepped in, representing the tying run. With strong hitters like Carter and Winfield to follow, Alomar was just hoping for a base hit or a walk to extend the rally. He did even better. Oakland reliever Dennis Eckersley put a fastball right over the middle of the plate and Alomar turned on it. As soon as he made contact, he knew he had gotten all of it. The ball sailed over the right-field fence for a two-run homer to tie the game.

The game went into extra innings, and the Blue Jays finally won, 7–6, in 11 innings. Alomar had four hits in the game, including his double to start a rally in the eighth and his home run to tie it in the ninth.

The Blue Jays were now within one win of the American League pennant.

Oakland avoided elimination with a win the next day, but the Blue Jays wrapped it up back in Toronto. Alomar had three hits in the game as Toronto won 9–2. This time there was good reason to celebrate.

For the first time ever, the World Series was coming to Canada, and Alomar was a big factor in its arrival. In the six games against Oakland, Alomar hit .423 with two home runs. For his performance, Alomar was named the Most Valuable Player of the American League Championship Series.

The Blue Jays' opponent in the World Series was the Atlanta Braves. The series was tied, one game each. The third game, played in Toronto, was tied 2–2 in the bottom of the ninth inning. Alomar led off with a single. He then stole second and later came home with the winning run on a single by Candy Maldonado. The Blue Jays won again the next night and were within a game of the world championship.

Atlanta won the fifth game to stay alive. Back in Atlanta for Game 6, the Blue Jays held a 2–1 lead in the last of the ninth. However, the Braves tied the game with two out to force the game into extra innings. Alomar was deeply disappointed. Toronto

Roberto Alomar and the Blue Jays were American League East champs in 1992, due in large part to Alomar's powerful hitting.

had been so close to winning the Series, and now they had more work to do.

Devon White of the Blue Jays was hit by a pitch to start the top of the 11th inning. Alomar then singled. After Joe Carter flied out, Dave Winfield drilled a double to left. White and Alomar scored on the play to put Toronto ahead by two runs. Atlanta rallied again in the bottom of the inning but came up short. The Blue Jays held on for a 4–3 win and were finally world champions.

The Alomar family celebrated in many places. Roberto's father watched the game from Arizona, where he was working at the Cubs's minor-league complex; Roberto's brother and his wife watched from their home in Cleveland (a few hours later the couple also celebrated the birth of a daughter); Roberto's mother watched from Salinas, Puerto Rico (where the streets were deserted since most of the other residents were also watching the game), and in Atlanta, Roberto celebrated most of all.

Normally Roberto Alomar would have returned to Puerto Rico right after the major-league season ended. This time he hung around for a couple of months in Toronto, where he was a huge hero. He made a lot of personal appearances and attended autograph sessions.

The Blue Jays were the talk of Toronto, and fans

expected another great season in 1993. They were not disappointed. The Blue Jays had the top three players in batting average in the American League: first baseman John Olerud led the league with a .363 average; designated hitter Paul Molitor, in his first season with Toronto after fifteen seasons with the Milwaukee Brewers, hit .332; Alomar was third with a .326 average.

Alomar also hit 17 home runs, scored 109 runs, and drove in 93 runs in addition to winning his third Gold Glove award at second base. (Alomar was the Gold Glove winner from 1991 through 1996.) He also was in the starting lineup in the All-Star Game for the third straight year. He hit a home run in the third inning that tied the game, helping lead the American League to a 9–3 win.

As for the Blue Jays, the team struggled early but moved into first place in late June. Toronto held the top spot for most of the rest of the season. However, six straight losses in early September left the Blue Jays clinging to a tie for first place with the New York Yankees. Finally the Blue Jays caught fire, winning nine in a row to open up a comfortable lead that they never gave up.

Toronto then beat the Chicago White Sox, four games to two, in the league playoffs to make it back to the World Series. Alomar hit .292 and stole four bases in the playoff series.

He added four more stolen bases in the World Series against the Philadelphia Phillies. It was a series that featured some wild games. Toronto won the fourth game, 15–14, after having been behind by five runs in the eighth inning.

The Blue Jays held a three-games-to-two lead going into the sixth game but trailed by a run in the last of the ninth. However, Joe Carter hit a home run with two runners aboard. It was a dramatic blast that gave the Blue Jays their second world championship in a row.

Alomar hit .480 (second-best among all players) in the six-game series and drove in six runs. Other players grabbed bigger headlines, but it was clear to Blue Jay fans who the number-one player on the team had been over the past few seasons.

Roberto Alomar was perhaps the best of the bunch on the top team in baseball.

Chapter 6

Rocky Roads

Playing on championship teams two years in a row was a high point in Roberto Alomar's career. There would be other high points, but there would be a few rough spots in between.

Following the 1993 season, Alomar played in the Puerto Rican League for the first time since the 1989–90 winter season. He did not last long, though. After just a few weeks, Alomar was trying to stretch a hit into a double when he caught his spikes in the hard dirt as he slid into second. In doing so, he broke his fibula, a bone in the leg, above his right ankle. That ended Alomar's winter season, and he returned to Toronto with his leg in a cast.

Fortunately he was ready to play when the 1994 major-league season opened. The major leagues would be using a new format that year. Instead of two divisions, both the American and National leagues would have three divisions: Eastern, Central, and Western. The three division champions in each league would advance to the playoffs along with the second-place team (called the wild-card team) with the best record.

Alomar had this to say about the new system: "I don't think a team that finishes in second place should get the chance to win it all. The point is to try to win first place."[1] The Toronto Blue Jays would play in the American League Eastern Division with the Baltimore Orioles, Boston Red Sox, Detroit Tigers, and New York Yankees.

Because the Blue Jays had won the World Series the previous two years, they were expected to do well again in 1994. They got off to a decent start but then had a disastrous month in May. They won just 10 of 26 games and were ten games out of first place at the end of the month. Things got worse in June when they lost ten straight games.

Alomar was having a good year again. His batting average was over .300, although he had a big decline in stolen bases. After having swiped 55 bases in 1993, he had only 19 in 1994. One of the reasons for the drop-off may have been because of the leg he broke. Another reason may have been that the season was shortened because of a strike by the players.

The players went on strike in August, with barely two thirds of the season completed. The strike wiped out the rest of the regular season as well as the playoffs. For some players and teams, it was devastating. A number of hitters had been having great years and had chances of setting some batting records. Those chances were denied because of the strike. Teams like the New York Yankees, who held a big lead in the American League East, were looking forward to getting to the playoffs for the first time in many years. Their dreams also ended.

For the Toronto Blue Jays, though, the early end to the season may have been a relief. They were in third place, 16 games out of first place. In general, though, the strike was a major blow to the game of baseball. However, it may have strengthened some of the winter leagues in the Caribbean in 1994–95. Major-league players were facing a long layoff because of the strike, and many who otherwise would have stayed on the mainland headed to the Caribbean to play ball.

Alomar had a new team to play for that winter. He had been traded by Ponce to the San Juan Senadores, a team that already had a number of star players like Carlos Baerga and Edgar Martinez.

FACT

In December 1994, Alomar teamed with Jose Oquendo, an infielder with the St. Louis Cardinals, in a charity doubles tennis match in Puerto Rico against a top-ranked women's doubles team of Gigi Fernandez and Natalia Zvereva. Proceeds from ticket sales from this match benefited the National Hispanic Scholarship Fund. While baseball may be Alomar's best sport, he enjoys participating in others such as tennis and basketball.

Bolstered by the addition of Alomar, the Senadores won the Puerto Rican League championship. For the second time, Alomar would be playing in the Caribbean Series, and this time he did not have far to go to do it. The 1995 Caribbean Series was played in San Juan.

Under rules of the series, the champions of each league are allowed to add a certain number of players from other teams in the league. For the Caribbean Series, the Senadores added outfielders Juan Gonzalez, Bernie Williams, and Ruben Sierra, along with pitchers Roberto Hernandez and Ricky Bones. Bones, who had made the American League All-Star team in 1994, said of the San Juan squad that would compete in the Caribbean Series, "This is the strongest team I have ever played with."[2]

Of course, the other teams would also be well stocked. The Venezuelan team, the Caracas Leones, had Omar Vizquel, one of the best fielding shortstops in baseball. The Este Azucareros of the Dominican Republic had Raul Mondesi, Henry Rodriguez, José Rijo, Pedro Martinez, Pedro Astacio, Mel Rojas, and Yorkis Perez.

San Juan had trouble in its first game, which was against the Hermosillo Naranjeros of the Mexican League. The Naranjeros jumped on Ricky Bones and built a 4–0 lead. But Alomar sparked a comeback with a three-run homer, and teammate Carlos Delgado tied the game with a solo shot. Later, Gonzalez and Baerga produced run-scoring singles to give San Juan a 6–5 win.

The Senadores beat the Caracas Leones in their next game and then prepared to meet the Dominican team, which had also won its first two games. Hiram Bithorn Stadium in San Juan was packed for the showdown. Fans expected a close game between these two great teams.

It was anything but close as the Senadores rolled to an easy 16–0 win over the Dominicans. Alomar had five hits in the game and drove in three runs.

San Juan then polished off the Mexican and Venezuelan teams and prepared to meet the Dominican team again. The Senadores at this point had a 5–0 record in the Caribbean Series while the Este Azucareros were 4–1. (Their only loss was the 16–0 drubbing at the hands of the Senadores.) If the Azucareros won the game, a tiebreaker game would have to be played to decide the championship. If the Senadores won, the series would be over.

José Rijo was on the mound for the Dominican team, and San Juan jumped on him early, scoring four runs in the first four innings. Meanwhile, Ricky Bones, the Senadores' starting pitcher, was unhittable. In fact, he carried a no-hitter into the sixth

In the winter of 1994 Alomar was traded by the Ponce Leones in the Puerto Rican League to the San Juan Senadores. His locker and uniform are shown here.

inning. San Juan won the game, 9–3, and captured the Caribbean Series Championship.

"We gave the fans a great show, and we won this for Puerto Rico," said Alomar, who had had a great series.[3] He led all batters with a .560 batting average with 10 RBIs and was named the Caribbean Series Most Valuable Player.

Things had gone better for Alomar in the Puerto Rican League that winter than they would with the Blue Jays in 1995. First, the season opened three weeks late because of the strike. Alomar was going into the final year of his contract with the Blue Jays. He had tried to get the team to discuss an extension to his contract, but the Blue Jays refused. Later in the year, when the team decided it wanted to talk about a long-term contract, Alomar refused. He had already given the Blue Jays a chance to sign him for several more seasons. At that point, he decided he would let his contract run out and become a free agent at the end of the year. He was considered one of the top players in the game and would be in demand by many teams.

Alomar was also concerned that the Blue Jays were not very committed to winning. He was having a good year himself. He did not make an error in the field until early July. He had gone 104 games without an error at second base—an American

The start of the 1995 season did not go smoothly for Alomar. The season started three weeks late due to a player strike, and Alomar decided he wanted to let his contract run out and be a free agent.

League record. He hit .300 for the fourth straight season and upped his stolen base total to 30.

But, as a team, the Blue Jays were floundering. Only two years before they had won the World Series. Now they were one of the worst teams in baseball. An eight-game losing streak in June dropped Toronto to last place in the American League East, where they stayed for most of the rest of the season.

Roberto's brother's team did better. The Cleveland Indians made it to the World Series for the first time in forty-one years. Roberto and his father went to the World Series games in Cleveland. No doubt Roberto would have rather been playing in the World Series than watching it. But he knew that was unlikely to happen again soon if he stayed with the Blue Jays. As a free agent, he could choose the team he wanted to play for. He wanted to make sure the team he chose was committed to winning, something he did not think was any longer the case with Toronto.

For the time being, though, he would concentrate on playing with the San Juan Senadores in the Puerto Rican League. With San Juan, Alomar ended up playing for his father once again. His father took over as the Senadores manager in December, during a time that the team was struggling. San Juan won

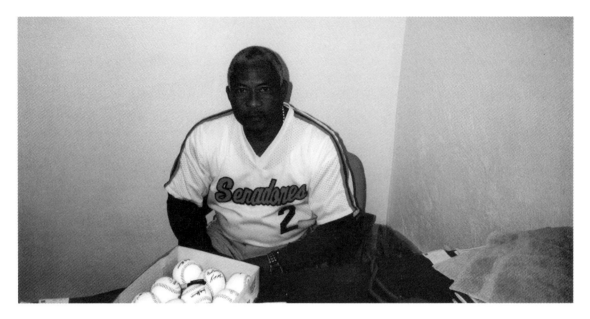

Sandy Alomar, Sr., (shown here) manages the same team on which Roberto Alomar plays during the winter—the San Juan Senadores.

six of its first eight games with Sandy Alomar, Sr., at the helm and was in the hunt for a playoff spot.

The fight for the playoffs went down to the wire as San Juan and Ponce battled for fourth place. At the same time, Alomar had a shot at winning the league's batting title. With two games left in the regular season, Alomar was trailing Rey Ordoñez of Santurce by 30 percentage points (.343 to .373). But Ordoñez went hitless in his final two games, and his batting averaged plummeted.

Alomar, on the other hand, finished the regular season with a surge. The Senadores tied with Ponce for fourth place and then beat the Leones in a tiebreaker game to grab the final playoff spot. In the final two scheduled games and the tiebreaker (which counted as part of the regular season), Alomar had 7 hits in 12 at-bats. He finished with a .362 average, more than ten points ahead of Ordoñez.

Alomar's hot finish made Roberto and his father only the second father and son to have won the Puerto Rican League batting championship. (Orlando and his father, Perucho Cepeda, were the first.)

San Juan did not do well in the playoffs and was quickly eliminated. The winter season over, Alomar prepared to return to major-league play, where he would be playing for a new team—the Baltimore Orioles.

As usual, he was looking forward to facing new challenges.

Chapter 7

New Challenges

The Baltimore Orioles were being picked by many experts to win the American League East in 1996. If that was not enough incentive for Alomar to join them, there was also the prospect of playing alongside Cal Ripken, Jr., one of the greatest shortstops in history and a true legend of the game. One of baseball's biggest stories in 1995 had been Ripken's breaking of Lou Gehrig's record for playing in the most consecutive games (2,130).

Ripken had not missed a game at shortstop for the Orioles since 1982. Over that time, he had played alongside many different second basemen. Just as Alomar looked forward to playing next to Ripken, Ripken looked forward to having a second baseman as good and as steady as Alomar.

Other Orioles were happy to see that they would have Alomar playing for, rather than against, them. First baseman Rafael Palmeiro pointed out that Alomar would no longer be able to rob him of base hits anymore. "My average went up ten points when we got him," said Palmeiro. "He stole at least five hits from me last year."[1]

The Orioles and Alomar got off to a great start in 1996. Baltimore won 11 of its first 13 games and opened up a four-game lead in the Eastern Division. The team cooled off a bit but stayed close to the top and moved back into first place for a couple of days near the end of May.

Meanwhile, Alomar was on fire. In mid-May he was leading the American League in batting average. By the end of the month, he had raised his average to over .400. No player in the major leagues had hit .400 for an entire season since Ted Williams hit .406 in 1941.

No one expected that Alomar would maintain that pace for the rest of the year, but he was off to an amazing start. He was doing it with his usual smooth stroke and sharp batting eye, but he was also doing it with his head. In a May 22 game against the Angels, the Orioles faced left-hander Jim Abbott. Normally the switch-hitting Alomar would bat right-handed against a lefty, but this time he did

When Roberto Alomar joined the Baltimore Orioles in 1996, many experts were picking the Orioles to win the American League East.

not. Abbott's best pitch is a slider that breaks in tightly on the fists of a right-handed hitter. Alomar felt he could handle the pitch more easily if he batted left-handed. He was right. He hit a single and a homer off Abbott and ended the game with four hits and three runs batted in.

"The more you see of Robbie, the more you appreciate him," said Cal Ripken. "He has an immense amount of ability. But he doesn't just try to get by on ability. He adds to it with knowledge."[2]

The season started in a great way for Alomar and the Orioles, but the good times did not last. Alomar's average did trail off, but he still finished the year hitting .328— his best batting average ever. He also won another Gold Glove.

However, the Orioles also cooled after their fast start and had to scramble for a playoff spot. Even though they were well out of first place, they had the chance to earn a wild-card spot as they went to Toronto for a series that would wrap up the regular season.

Alomar seemed to snap in the first game of the series. In the first inning, he was called out on strikes by home plate umpire John Hirschbeck. Alomar did not like the call and a heated argument followed. Alomar alleged that Hirschbeck swore at him. He tried to get at the umpire but was held back by teammates. Alomar then spit at the umpire.

Alomar was kicked out of the game, and the American League suspended him for five games. He appealed the suspension. He knew what he did was wrong, but he at least wanted a hearing so that he could continue playing in the heat of the race. Eventually Alomar issued an apology. The incident showed that anyone can make a mistake.

Since he appealed, the suspension would not begin immediately. Alomar was in the lineup the next afternoon. The Orioles were glad to have him. They needed a win to clinch a wild-card berth for the playoffs. On the other hand, the fans in Toronto were not happy to see Alomar. Because of the incident the night before, Alomar was booed—by the same Toronto fans who used to cheer him—every time he came up to bat. The game was tied 2–2 and went into extra innings. But in the tenth inning, Alomar hit a home run to center field to win the game. The win clinched the wild-card playoff spot for the Orioles.

But making the playoffs only served to continue the controversy. The umpires were unhappy that Alomar's suspension had not yet begun and threatened to boycott the playoff games. Alomar finally announced he would drop his appeal, and the

American League announced that his suspension would take place at the beginning of the 1997 season.

Alomar was still able to play as the Orioles faced the Cleveland Indians in the first round of the playoffs. The fans in Cleveland were no kinder than those in Toronto. They booed and jeered Alomar as much as they could.

The Orioles led two games to one and were within one game of winning the playoff series. The fourth game was in Cleveland, and the Indians held a 3–2 lead in the ninth inning. Baltimore had the tying run on second base, but there were two out. Alomar stepped in and, ignoring the boos, calmly stroked a single to center to tie the game.

That did not silence the Cleveland fans, but what Alomar did his next time up pretty well quieted them. In the 12th inning, Alomar hit a home run to center field to put Baltimore ahead 4–3. The Orioles held on to win and capture the playoff series from Cleveland.

That was as far as the Orioles went. They were eliminated by the New York Yankees in the League Championship Series, and their season came to an end. It was a draining finish for Alomar. He had used poor judgment and faced hostile audiences; still, he maintained his composure and came through in clutch situations.

FACT

Following the spitting incident with umpire John Hirschbeck, Alomar made a donation of fifty thousand dollars for adrenoleukodystrophy (ALD). One of umpire Hirschbeck's sons died of ALD, and his other son has the disease. Alomar's contribution, which was matched by the Baltimore Orioles, helped finance a major breakthrough in research to fight the disease.[3]

Alomar was booed by the fans in the first game he played following the "spitting incident" with umpire John Hirschbeck. However, in the tenth inning he hit a home run to win the game.

FACT

Fans from the mainland will notice differences in games they watch in the Puerto Rican League. There is little pregame fanfare. No type of anthem is played before the game; the teams just take the field and start playing. Photographers are on the field during the game, stationed in foul territory. And instead of a player's name being above his number on the back of his jersey, this space is used for advertising. Each team has a sponsor, whose name appears above or below the number on the jersey.

Alomar was happier than usual to get back to Puerto Rico after the season. There, he was at home and could play in peace. For the second straight winter, he was among the league leaders in batting average, and he hoped he could capture a second consecutive batting title.

He held the lead in mid-December with a .353 average but then had a couple of hitless games. On December 14, though, he came back with three hits and three RBIs in a 7–1 win over the Mayaguez Indios. This raised his average to .356 and put him back in the lead. Wil Cordero, the second baseman for the Indios, was hitless in four at-bats in the game. Cordero's performance was significant because the batting race turned out to be between Alomar and Cordero.

The race for the playoffs also went to the end. San Juan won 14 of its final 20 regular-season games to tie the Arecibo Lobos for fourth place and the final playoff spot, forcing a tiebreaker game. Alomar had a .009 lead over Cordero (.353 to .344) at this point but needed at least one hit if he was going to hold the lead and win the title. He got that hit in the first inning. It was a two-run homer that put the Senadores ahead to stay. San Juan made the playoffs, and Alomar, who finished the season with a .347 average, had his second straight batting championship.

San Juan swept past Santurce in the opening playoff round but then lost to the Mayaguez Indios for the Puerto Rican League championship. The Indios would advance to the Caribbean Series, to be played in Hermosillo, Mexico, and Alomar would be with them. Mayaguez was able to add players from other Puerto Rican League teams to their roster, and Alomar was one whom they chose.

Even though Alomar was not a regular member of the Mayaguez team, he was recognized as the best player in the series. He was also the most popular among young fans looking for autographs and reporters seeking interviews.

Mayaguez won its first game against the Aguilas Cibaeñas of the Dominican Republic but then lost its next four games. The Cibaeñas, after losing their first two games, went on to win their next four to capture the series.

It had been a satisfying winter for Alomar, winning a batting championship and playing in the Caribbean Series. But then trouble hit again. He played in a charity basketball game in Puerto Rico and injured his left ankle, spraining and chipping it. When he arrived for spring training with the

Orioles, he was on crutches and expected to miss several weeks.

Alomar also had to serve his five-game suspension at the start of the 1997 season. He did, however, shake hands with umpire Hirschbeck at the start of the season—a meaningful resolution to a bad incident. He then struggled at the plate for a few weeks before breaking out with the three-homer game against Boston.

He picked up the pace, raising his batting average to over .300 in June, and was voted by the fans to be the starting second baseman in the All-Star Game. The game would be in Cleveland, and his brother would also be in it. It turned out to be a sad time for the Alomars. Back in Puerto Rico, the brothers' grandmother had died the week before. But Roberto and his brother were happy to be on the same team again, even if for only one day, and it turned out to be a big night for both.

Even though Roberto Alomar had no hits, he made a fine play in the field to help preserve an American League lead in the early innings. The National League later tied the game, but Roberto's brother hit a two-run homer in the seventh inning to give the American League a 3–1 win. Thanks to the big blow, Sandy Alomar was named the game's Most Valuable Player. After the game, Roberto said,

Following a five-game suspension at the start of the 1997 season, Alomar struggled at the plate for a few weeks.

"Our family has been through a lot. To see my brother hit that home run is such a great feeling. This is one of the happiest days of my life."[4]

Alomar had a great time in the All-Star Game, but he was happy to get back to the regular season, especially since his team was doing so well. The Orioles had a win-loss record of 55–33 at the All-Star break and were in first place in the American League Eastern Division, seven games ahead of the New York Yankees.

The Orioles stayed in first place for the rest of the season and won the American League East title. However, it was still a difficult year for Alomar. He suffered a groin injury near the end of July and barely played until the second week in September. But he returned from the injury in spectacular fashion. He hit .515 in his final 18 games of the regular season and raised his batting average from .297 to .333.

In the opening round of the playoffs, Alomar had only three hits, but one of them was a big one. It was a two-run double that put the Orioles ahead to stay in the second game. Baltimore defeated Seattle, three games to one, and advanced to the League Championship Series. Unfortunately, for the second straight year, the Orioles fell one step short of the World Series. They were defeated, four games to

Roberto Alomar and his brother, Sandy Alomar, Jr., were on the same team for one day in the All-Star Game of 1997. But Roberto was happy to return to the regular season with the Orioles—who were in first place in the American League East.

two, by the Cleveland Indians in the American League Championship Series.

An Alomar would be in the World Series, but once again it would be Roberto's brother, as a member of the Indians. Roberto would be pulling for his brother but wishing he were there instead.

Roberto Alomar returned home to Puerto Rico, where he remained as focused as ever on baseball. But there he has a separate life. He plays tennis and volleyball and also enjoys walking on the beach, listening to music, and puttering around on a miniature golf course. He allows himself to relax and think about how lucky he is.

> I see children in wheelchairs, and they go through life with a smile on their faces. We have all the pieces, and sometimes we go through life without a smile on the face. We don't realize how good we have it.
>
> My dad always told me, "Roberto, the way to be successful, go out there and have some fun. If you are not enjoying it and don't have a smile on your face, don't do it."[5]

Alomar did well again in 1998, despite the fact that his team did not perform well. The Orioles were expected to contend for the title in the American League Eastern Division. However, near the end of April, the team was stuck in fourth place with little hope of making the playoffs.

Alomar was keeping his batting average around .300 and was among the team leaders in doubles and runs scored by mid-season. He also started in the All-Star Game. He had 3 hits and 2 runs in the American League's 13–8 win. For his outstanding performance, Alomar was named the Most Valuable Player in the game.

Chapter 8

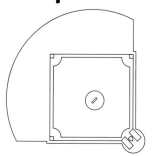

Born to Play Baseball

Roberto Alomar was born into a baseball culture. This culture extended to his family with a father and several uncles who were pro ballplayers. But the culture also extended to his homeland.

Puerto Rico is an island approximately one thousand miles to the southeast of Florida. Although it covers only 3,435 square miles—it is smaller than the state of Connecticut—the island provides a dividing place between the Atlantic Ocean to the north and the Caribbean Sea to the south. Its name, Spanish for "rich port," symbolizes the island's bounty of exportable products such as sugarcane and coffee.

In 1898, Puerto Rico became a possession of the United States. It now has the status of being a

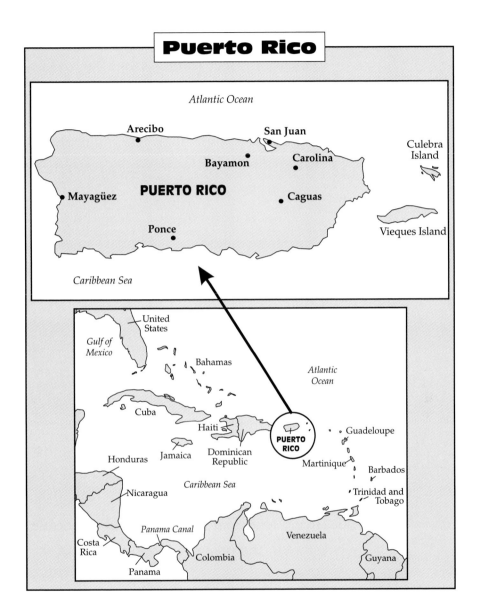

Puerto Rico

Atlantic Ocean

Arecibo

San Juan

Culebra
Island

Bayamon

Carolina

PUERTO RICO

Mayagüez

Caguas

Vieques Island

Ponce

Caribbean Sea

United
States

Gulf of
Mexico

Bahamas

Atlantic
Ocean

Cuba

Haiti

Guadeloupe

PUERTO
RICO

Honduras

Jamaica

Dominican
Republic

Martinique

Barbados

Nicaragua

Caribbean Sea

Trinidad and
Tobago

Costa
Rica

Panama Canal

Venezuela

Colombia

Guyana

Panama

As citizens of the United States, Puerto Ricans share not only their citizenship, but also their love of baseball with mainland citizens.

United States Commonwealth. A commonwealth is not a state like Michigan or Hawaii. It does elect a governor just as states do, but Puerto Ricans cannot vote for the president of the United States. Also, the residents of Puerto Rico are citizens of the United States, although they maintain much of their Spanish heritage from the time that the island was ruled by Spain.

One feature Puerto Ricans share with their Caribbean neighbors is a love of baseball. These islands and countries have produced a number of fine baseball players. A look at major-league baseball rosters today will reveal many players, a lot of great stars among them, who are Latin American.

Baseball in Puerto Rico goes back to about the time that the island became a part of the United States. For many years, no one on the island played for money. They were all amateur players. That changed in 1938 when the Puerto Rican League began. It is a professional league that has operated every winter since then. A lot of players who became stars in the major leagues on the mainland United States got their start in the Puerto Rican League. In 1942, Hiram Bithorn became the first Puerto Rican to play in the major leagues when he pitched for the Chicago Cubs.

Bithorn had an advantage over a lot of other

Puerto Ricans. He was light-skinned. At the time black players—whether they were African Americans or dark-skinned Latin Americans—were not allowed to play in the majors. Because of this, one of Puerto Rico's best players, Pedro "Perucho" Cepeda, never got to play in the major leagues.

Even for Latin players who were light-skinned like Bithorn, it was a difficult road. If they did not speak English, they had trouble communicating in the United States. There were also a lot of unfair attitudes toward Latin Americans. "Latin players learned they could be easily branded as lazy," says Peter C. Bjarkman, author of *Baseball with a Latin Beat: A History of the Latin American Game.* "As a result, they had to work harder than other players. A player from the mainland might be able to sit out a game if he was injured or not feeling well. If a Latin player did this, there was a better chance someone might think he was faking an injury."[1] Things are better today for Latin-American players. Many more are playing in the majors. A Latin player may have several teammates who speak his native language and understand his culture. Of course, it also no longer matters if a player's skin is white or black.

The color barrier existed for many years in organized baseball—that is, in the American and

Hiram Bithorn (whose statue and plaque are shown in front of the stadium named after him in Puerto Rico) was the first Puerto Rican to play in the major leagues.

National leagues and their affiliated minor leagues. It was finally broken in the mid-1940s by Jackie Robinson, who was black. Robinson played in 1946 for the Montreal Royals, a minor-league team. The following year he joined the Brooklyn Dodgers (now the Los Angeles Dodgers) and became the first African American to play in the majors in more than sixty years. Robinson opened the door for other black players, including Puerto Ricans like Orlando Cepeda (Perucho's son) and Roberto Clemente.

Cepeda had an outstanding career, hitting 379 home runs over seventeen major-league seasons. In 1967, as a member of the St. Louis Cardinals, Cepeda won the National League's Most Valuable Player (MVP) award.

Roberto Clemente, son of a sugarcane worker in the Puerto Rican village of Carolina, became a great star in the majors and was the first Latin-American player ever inducted into Baseball's Hall of Fame. Clemente amassed 3,000 hits while playing for the Pittsburgh Pirates and was one of the best outfielders in the National League in the 1960s. He was known for his strong throwing arm. He won the National League MVP award in 1966, the year before Cepeda. Clemente was just as well known for his humanitarian activities. He spoke out and fought for the rights of Latin-American players. He also helped others, and that led to his death. On New Year's Eve in 1972, Clemente died in a plane crash while transporting supplies to earthquake-stricken Nicaragua.

Many of these players, even though they could now play in major-league baseball, still played in the Puerto Rican League. They would come home each winter and play on one of the teams. It was a way to make a little more money (baseball players were not paid nearly as much back then as they are now) and stay in shape over the winter. But it was also the only chance for many of the people of Puerto Rico to watch them play. Few Puerto Ricans were able to see Roberto Clemente play in person for the Pittsburgh Pirates. But they could watch him as a member of the Santurce Cangrejeros. Clemente started playing winter ball in Puerto Rico before he signed his first pro contract on the mainland. And he continued playing winter ball well past the time that he needed the money or even a way to keep his batting eye sharp. He felt an obligation to the people of Puerto Rico. Clemente was perhaps the greatest hero the island has ever known, and he took that responsibility seriously. Youngsters in Puerto Rico, just like those on the mainland, look up to baseball players as their heroes. Sandy Alomar, Sr., looked up to players like Roberto Clemente while growing up in the 1950s. But he remembers an even greater Puerto Rican player than Clemente.

FACT

For many players, the Puerto Rican League was a place to sharpen their skills. Players such as Mike Schmidt, a great slugger, and Rickey Henderson, the best base stealer ever, both credit their experience in the Puerto Rican League with helping them reach new heights in the major leagues. The Puerto Rican League has been referred to as baseball's launching pad because of the development it provided for aspiring players such as these.

Victor Pellot (pronounced Pay-yo) was breaking into organized ball around the same time as Clemente. Pellot was a first baseman but could play a variety of positions in the infield and outfield. On the mainland, Pellot played under a different name—Vic Power. Sandy Alomar, Sr., said Pellot (Power) was the best player Puerto Rico ever produced. "I start[ed] a few arguments by saying that," claimed Alomar. "Clemente was the best hitter and the best outfielder, but Power was the best player we ever had. He played many positions and played them well. He could play any position with grace, and he was very smart."[2]

Roberto Alomar's father admired Orlando Cepeda and Victor Pellot as he played in youth leagues while growing up in the southern part of Puerto Rico. But he also had some heroes in his own family, older brothers who were playing pro ball on the mainland. Alomar joined them in 1960, when at the age of sixteen, he signed a contract with the Milwaukee (now Atlanta) Braves.

Alomar went to the mainland during his two-month vacation from high school. He spent the summer working out but not playing with the Braves' minor-league team in Wellsville, New York. His brother, Demitrio, was playing there. Wellsville was in the New York-Penn League, a Class-D

FACT

Puerto Rico is sometimes called an island nation, but it is really not a nation at all. For several centuries it was ruled by Spain and was a colony of that European country. Puerto Rico occupied a strategic spot in the Caribbean as Spain battled other European nations for domination in the Western Hemisphere. Wars and battles were fought on and around Puerto Rico. The island also served as a secret hiding place for pirates and smugglers, another part of its rich and colorful history.

league. Major-league teams have a number of minor-league clubs, called farm teams, at a variety of levels. Class-D was the lowest level, a place for players just getting started.

The following year, Alomar returned during his school vacation and played shortstop for another Class-D team in Davenport, Iowa. Finally in 1962, after he graduated from high school, Alomar was able to concentrate more on baseball as he worked his way up the Braves's minor-league ladder. After the season on the mainland ended, he came home and played in the Puerto Rican League.

The senior Alomar's brothers were also playing in minor-league systems with the hope of reaching the majors. His twin brothers, Rafael and Tony, both reached the Triple-A level, only a step away from the majors. Unfortunately for them, they never made that final jump to the majors. Things worked out better for Sandy. He was called up by the Braves in September of 1964 and then made the team's opening-day roster in 1965. At that point, he switched from shortstop to second base. That's the position he usually played, but—like his hero, Victor Pellot—he learned to be versatile. He ended up spending fifteen seasons in the major leagues and played every position but pitcher and catcher.

He learned another skill that helped him play

Sandy Alomar, Sr., is shown here in his days with the Mets. He got his start in the Puerto Rican League, however.

regularly. He became a switch-hitter. Around the time Alomar was getting started in organized ball, managers were beginning to platoon players. That means they would fill their lineup with more left-handed hitters when a right-handed pitcher was starting for the other team. They would load up with right-handed hitters against a left-handed pitcher. Alomar knew his key to being a regular player was to hit from both sides of the plate. He tried switch-hitting while in the minors in 1964 but was told to stop. He picked it up again a few years later and stuck with it throughout his career. It paid off as it helped him to earn a regular spot in the line-up. While a member of the California (now Anaheim) Angels in the early 1970s, Alomar played in 648 consecutive games.

In Puerto Rico, the name Alomar would continue to be synonymous with baseball.

Chapter Notes

Chapter 1. Focus on Baseball

1. ESPNET SportsZone <http://espnet. sportszone.com/mlb/970426/recap/bosbal.html>.

2. Amy Shipley, "Alomar's Power Trip Propels Orioles, 14–5," *Washington Post*, April 27, 1997, p. D1.

Chapter 2. Childhood Years

1. Author interview with Sandy Alomar, Sr., San Juan, Puerto Rico, December 12, 1996.

2. Ibid.

3. Daniel P. George, "Tops in Toronto," *Boys' Life*, April 1994, p. 9.

4. Author interview with Sandy Alomar, Sr., San Juan, Puerto Rico, December 12, 1996.

Chapter 3. Baseball Throughout the Year

1. Stephen Brunt, *Second to None: The Roberto Alomar Story* (New York: Viking Press, 1993), p. 64.

Chapter 4. Pride of the Padres

1. Bruce Newman, "Home Suite Home," *Sports Illustrated*, June 8, 1992, p. 39.

Chapter 5. Reaching the Top

No notes.

Chapter 6. Rocky Roads

1. Lisa Winston, "Two Minutes with Roberto Alomar," *USA Today Baseball Weekly*, April 20–26, 1994, p. 16.

2. Tony Menendez, "Puerto Rico, Mexico Titles Go to Repeaters; 'Dream Teams' Vie in Caribbean Series," *USA Today Baseball Weekly*, February 8–21, 1995, p. 35.

3. Tony Menendez, "Puerto Rico's 'Dream Team' Prevails: Alomar Leads Series Sweep," *USA Today Baseball Weekly*, February 22–28, 1995, p. 28

Chapter 7. New Challenges.

1. Thomas Boswell, "Keep an Eye on the Turn-Style," *The Sporting News*, March 11, 1996, p. 9.

2. Mark Maske, ".401: With a Batting Average Second to None, Orioles' Alomar a Huge Hit All Around," *Washington Post*, May 28, 1996, p. C1.

3. Bill Koenig, "Sibling Revelry," *USA Today Baseball Weekly*, July 16, 1997, p. 28.

4. Patrick Reusse, "Alomars Sparkle for AL Stars," *Minneapolis Star Tribune*, July 9, 1997, p. C1.

5. Erik Brady, "For the Alomars, Baseball Remains a Family Affair," *Baseball Digest*, September 1996, p. 23

Chapter 8. Born to Play Baseball

1. Peter C. Bjarkman, *Baseball with a Latin Beat: A History of the Latin American Game* (Jefferson, N.C.: McFarland & Company, Inc., 1994), p. 56.

2. Author interview with Sandy Alomar, Sr., San Juan, Puerto Rico, December 12, 1996.

Career Statistics

Year	Team	G	AB	R	H	2B	3B	HR	RBI	BB	SB	Avg
1988	San Diego	143	545	84	145	24	6	9	41	47	24	.266
1989	San Diego	158	623	82	184	27	1	7	56	53	42	.295
1990	San Diego	147	586	80	168	27	5	6	60	48	24	.287
1991	Toronto	161	637	88	188	41	11	9	69	57	53	.295
1992	Toronto	152	571	105	177	27	8	8	76	87	49	.310
1993	Toronto	153	589	109	192	35	6	17	93	80	55	.326
1994	Toronto	107	392	78	120	25	4	8	38	51	19	.306
1995	Toronto	130	517	71	155	24	7	13	66	47	30	.300
1996	Baltimore	153	588	132	193	43	4	22	94	90	17	.328
1997	Baltimore	112	412	64	137	23	2	14	60	40	9	.333
Totals		1,416	5,460	893	1,659	296	54	113	653	600	322	.304

G—Games
AB—At-Bats
R—Runs
H—Hits
2B—Doubles
3B—Triples

HR—Home Runs
RBI—Runs Batted In
BB—Bases on Balls
SB—Stolen Bases
Avg—Batting Average

Where to Write
Roberto Alomar

Mr. Roberto Alomar
c/o Baltimore Orioles
Oriole Park at Camden Yards
333 W. Camden Street
Baltimore, MD 21201

On the Internet at:

http://cbs.sportsline.com/u/baseball/mlb/players/
http://cgi.cnnsi.com/baseball/mlb/ml/players/Roberto.Alomar/

Index

A

Abbott, Jim, 70, 72
Aguilas Cibaeñas, 77
Alomar, Demitrio (uncle), 90
Alomar, Maria (mother), 11,
    25, 53
Alomar, Rafael (uncle), 91
Alomar, Sandy Jr., (brother),
    11, 12, 14, 16, 17, 20,
    25, 26, 28, 36, 46, 47,
    53, 65, 78
Alomar, Sandy Sr., (father),
    11, 12, 13 ,14, 16, 17,
    20, 25, 29, 34, 53, 65,
    66, 89, 90, 91, 92, 93
Alomar, Tony (uncle), 91
Alou, Felipe, 26
Anderson, Brady, 9
Arecibo Lobos, 76
Astacio, Pedro, 60
Atlanta Braves, 51, 53

B

Baerga, Carlos, 29, 59, 61
Baltimore Orioles, 7–9, 58,
    67, 69-74, 78, 80
Bithorn, Hiram, 85, 86, 87
Bones, Ricky, 60, 61
Bordick, Mike, 7–8
Boston Red Sox, 7–8, 44, 58,
    78
Bowa, Larry, 29, 33
Brooklyn Dodgers, 88

C

Caguas Criollos, 26, 27–28,
    33, 34
California Angels, 12, 93
Caracas Leones, 60, 61

Carter, Joe, 37, 47, 48, 50, 53,
    55
Cepeda, Orlando, 67, 88, 90
Cepeda, Pedro "Perucho,"
    67, 86
Charleston Rainbows, 23–25
Chicago Cubs, 36, 37, 85
Chicago White Sox, 54
Cincinnati Reds, 19
Clemente, Roberto, 88, 89
Cleveland Indians, 65, 74, 82
Cordero, Wil, 76

D

Delgado, Carlos, 61
Detroit Tigers, 58

E

Este Azucareros, 60, 61
Eckersley, Dennis, 50

F

Fernandez, Gigi, 59
Fernandez, Tony, 37
Flannery, Tim, 29

G

Gehrig, Lou, 69
Gillick, Pat, 46
Gonzalez, Juan, 34, 60, 61
Gwynn, Tony, 29, 33, 34

H

Hawkins, Andy, 33
Henderson, Rickey, 89
Hermosillo Naranjeros, 60,
    61
Hernandez, Roberto, 60
Hirschbeck, John, 72–73, 74,
    75, 78

Houston Astros, 31–33

L

Las Vegas Stars, 30, 31
Los Angeles Dodgers, 31

M

Maldonado, Candy, 51
Martinez, Edgar, 59
Martinez, Pedro, 60
Mayaguez Indios, 76, 77
McGriff, Fred, 37
McKeon, Jack, 33, 36
Milwaukee Braves, 90
Minnesota Twins, 44, 46
Molitor, Paul, 54
Mondesi, Raul, 50
Montreal Royals, 88
Morris, Jack, 46, 48

N

Newman, Al, 26
New York Mets, 92
New York Yankees, 19, 54, 58, 59, 74, 80

O

Oakland Athletics, 50–51
Olerud, John, 54
Oquendo, Jose, 59
Ordoñez, Rey, 66, 67

P

Palmiero, Rafael, 70
Pellot, Victor, 90, 91
Perez, Yorkis, 60
Philadelphia Phillies, 55
Ponce Leones, 14, 16, 34, 35, 59, 66
Power, Vic, *See also*, Victor Pellot

R

Ready, Randy, 29
Reno Silver Sox, 27

Riddoch, Greg, 36–37, 41
Rijo, José, 60, 61
Ripken, Cal, Jr., 9, 69, 72
Robinson, Jackie, 88
Rodriguez, Henry, 60
Rojas, Mel, 60
Rosa, Luis, 18, 20, 29
Ryan, Nolan, 31–32, 42

S

San Diego Padres, 18, 20, 29–30, 31–39
Sandberg, Ryne, 36
San Francisco Giants, 34
San Juan Senadores, 59–63, 65, 66, 67, 76–77
Santiago, Benito, 32
Santurce Cangrejeros, 77
Schmidt, Mike, 89
Seattle Mariners, 80
Sierra, Ruben, 60

T

Templeton, Garry, 28
Texas Rangers, 42
Thon, Dickie, 32
Toronto Blue Jays, 37–39, 41–59, 63–65, 72, 73
Toronto Maple Leafs, 39, 44

V

Vizquel, Omar, 60

W

White, Devon, 50, 53
Wichita Wranglers, 28
Williams, Bernie, 60
Williams, Ted, 70
Winfield, Dave, 46, 48, 50, 53
Wynne, Marvell, 32

Z

Zvereva, Natalia, 59